In 1990 Linda Baxter gave up teaching Modern Languages in order to write, but suffered a subarachnoid haemorrhage which damaged the language centre of her brain. She began the slow and arduous process of re-learning her mother tongue. In 1996 she moved to Wales and found the inspiration to write again. When her son Timo was murdered writing became a release valve for her grief, pain and anger. *Losing Timo* is her first full-length published work.

*I never knew that my love for my son went to such depths of my being.*

*to Susan*

# LOSING
# TIMO

by

Linda Baxter

*Linda Baxter*

*October 2004*

HONNO AUTOBIOGRAPHY

*Published by Honno*
*'Ailsa Craig', Heol y Cawl, Dinas Powys*
*Bro Morgannwg, CF6 4AH*

First impression 2004

British Library Cataloguing in Publication Data.

A catalogue record for this book is available from the British Library.

ISBN 1 870206 66 5

*Published with the financial support of the Welsh Books Council*

Cover design by Chris Lee Design

*Cover photographs:*
The front cover combines two images: above, a detail
from the memorial bench made by Eifion Thomas;
below, a view from the Baxters' home in west Wales.

Back cover image: Timo skateboarding outside
the Baxters' house in Barnes, 1991.

Typeset and printed in Wales by
Dinefwr Press, Llandybïe.

# Contents

# PROLOGUE

Dear Timo

After nine weeks of waiting we can at last put you to rest in the dell at bottom of the far field. Your blackened, skin-slipped body couldn't be dressed, but we put the clothes in the coffin anyway – black ones! – with the ginkgo sweat-shirt, and the spare glasses. Mr Jones has given me a lock of your hair, which I've put in your Indian trinket box to go with your photos and the finger skateboard and Grandma's Raoul bowl, and the birthday cards you sent us this year, on the sideboard in the conservatory.

The coffin is very special – it's a wicker basket, made just for you by a back-to-the-old-days chap who lives in the woods somewhere in Sir Gaerfyrddin. It's a dark wicker, done up with white satin. When we lower you into the grave, we're going to cover you with blue and orange flowers – the same colour as at the Memorial – and yellow and white flowers as well. My letter and poem, and Auntie Fan's letter, and Amanda's poem, and Sam's message we shall put in an old-days black metal moneybox, and do it up with a blue velvet bow, and we shall put that in the grave too, along with the mementoes that people have brought. We shall think of the people who cannot be here today, and throw in a flower especially for them. Then we shall say a poem together: 'Do not stand at my grave and weep'. Hope you approve. At the end we shall each throw some soil into your grave. And we shall plant a whispering aspen poplar by your side.

I shall never forgive those mindless thugs, those six small pieces of squeaking arse-pit, for what they did to you on that Friday, for what they did to us.

No more phone calls, no more visits back and forth, we shan't see you become the successful, altruistic lawyer, no grandchildren to take down to Cwm-yr-Eglwys or Aber-fforest, no hide and seek in the bracken, no ponies . . .

It should have been the other way round. You should have been burying us in this field. As it is, we shall join you later – me, and Dizney, and Hermann, and Schnuss. We loved you, we do love you, deeply and terribly and so much. Sam and I are proud to be your parents, proud to have had a son who was, and still is, so respected, so esteemed, so loved, by so many people.

I can't hug you, kiss you, say take care and drive carefully and ring as soon as you get back. I'm meant to say goodbye Timo; but instead I'll read out my first Timo poem, the one I read at the Memorial, when you weren't with us. The spark was the memory of a particular visit to the baby clinic, an early example of you making me a proud mother. Do you remember being shown a picture of a bus? – a red bus – nothing else on the page but a stationary red bus? The doctor expected you to say: BUS! But you thought for a bit and then said:

### That Red Bus Has Stopped

The early talker did not just say bus; the
philosophiser saw it was not moving
(and was red). The natural linguist BMXed to
skating, ollies over bollards, grinding,
ankles needing frozen peas, reaction
to the decks, the headphones, elemental
gliding, singular fulfilment – no airs:
embarrassed by privilege, he did his own despite . . .

He took dysphasic mother walkies, shopping,
checked her spellings, dogsat Hermann, brought
the Heimat book, the Hendrix tape, Italian

deli, stacked the dishwasher. Two hundred
and fifty miles to phone on a Friday.
*Hello Mum . . .*

        that red bus has stopped.

                    Lots of love always
                            Mum

                        + S + H + Ss

# INTRODUCTION

# Timothy Raoul Baxter

## 17 January 1975 – 18 June 1999

Timo was born and brought up in London. He was our only child. In 1996, when Timo was nearing the end of his studies at Manchester University, we moved the family home to west Wales. Sam had a new job and a new impetus in his work; I was beginning to renovate my life after a brain haemorrhage. After he graduated, Timo preferred to live with his friends in London. I never worried. He had a large number of friends; my sister and brother-in-law, Fan and Nigel, who had no children of their own, were very fond of him, and would provide a family base at their home in Notting Hill. At Easter 1999 – the last time we saw him alive – he told us of his decision to pursue a career in law. He was due to start at the College of Law in London in September 1999.

On Saturday 12 June 1999 the lease on the flat in Mile End that he had been sharing expired. He made temporary arrangements to share a room with a friend in East Dulwich. Most of his belongings he stored at Fan and Nigel's house. On Tuesday 15 June he rang to say that he would be coming to stay for a while on the following Monday, and gave me his new address and telephone number. He also said that he would be going to an Open Day at the College of Law on Friday. I usually phoned him on a Friday morning. Fine, I said, I'll ring you over the weekend.

# The First Few Days

At around 2pm the policeman arrived at our house. I had been getting Timo's room ready.

My immediate fear was that something had happened to Sam. But Police Constable Mike Jones from Fishguard asked me straight away if Sam was at home. He told me that Timo was missing. That Timo's friend Gabriel had been rescued from the River Thames early that morning after an incident on a bridge. Gabriel had said that Timo had been with him.

Sam came home and PC Jones telephoned Detective Constable Susan Bishop at Paddington Police Station. She was to be our Family Liaison Officer. She said that Gabriel was in St Thomas's Hospital, rather confused. He had been in the water for something like forty minutes, he had had a nasty bang on the head. His stepfather was with him. Gabriel had said that he and Timo had been crossing Hungerford Bridge on their way to Gabriel's flat in the Oxo Tower on the South Bank in the early morning. A group of muggers had appeared and there was a fracas. Gabriel was pushed into the river. He did not know what had happened to Timo. Two people were in custody. CCTV tapes would show potential witnesses. Five friends had been to the police station to see if they could help. Timo might be wandering around the streets in a concussed state and might eventually turn up in hospital. The police were in touch with all the hospitals in case this should happen. He might be in the water. The river police were looking for him. The worst scenario would be that he had drowned. If that was the case, it would take anything from three to seven days for his body to be washed up on shore.

After PC Jones left I phoned Fan and Nigel. They cancelled their dinner engagement to be on hand should there be any news. Sam phoned his brother, Martin, in West Yorkshire. Castlepride Kennels would leave their unlocked van outside their house in case we had to leave the dogs and drive to London in the middle of the night.

*Saturday 19 June 1999*

Timo still had not been found by this morning. We knew he had to be dead. His body was recovered from the south foreshore of the Thames, at Gabriel's Wharf, that afternoon.

We took Hermann and Schnuss to the kennels and drove to Notting Hill. It was about 8pm. We had cups of tea and Nigel rang Paddington Police Station to say that we were here. Sue Bishop and Detective Inspector Dermot Keating arrived very fast. More cups of tea. These police persons were much better than I had expected. They talked and explained. They now had three in custody: one was only 16 years old. There were three more to be caught. They suggested that Sam and I might prefer someone else to go to the morgue for the identification. Timo did not look very nice. Perhaps we could get a friend to go? Sue had been impressed by the five friends who had been to the station yesterday. Maybe one, or a couple of them could go in our stead. We did not feel we could ask them to do something that was distasteful and upsetting and downright awful. It was our duty. Our right somehow. Dermot was not impressed and brought out some polaroids – but were we sure we wanted to see them? We dared, and he looked swollen, bloated, in the dark somehow, and every bit as ghastly and dead as I had imagined. So we insisted on going.

He did not look as bad as in the pictures. Less swollen, less bloated. Injured, but Timo. Ghastly and dead. Cried and cried. They had covered him in a purple drape with brocade trimmings, rather churchy. I thought we would be able to see him in his clothes, just as they had fished him out. Sue said she would see what she could do. It was bad not being able to touch him. He was behind a glass screen. There was going to be a post-mortem.

*Sunday 20 June 1999*

In the morning we inspected Timo's belongings in Fan and Nigel's coal hole: the computer that Nigel had given him, the books he had had in Burdett Road, bedding, knick-knacks and Indian stuff (including that huge reefer pot), a large number of skateboard videos and magazines, snow-boarding gear, two decks, two speakers, two boxes of records, university notes, a dartboard, cooking items, posters.

In the afternoon we went round to Timo's best friend's house in Barnes. Wept with Fin at the door. Most of the main friends were there, twenty-one of them. Everybody quiet, devastated. We sat round the big table with cups of tea. I was being efficient, had an agenda: (1) statement to the police about Timo, (2) views on possessions – to whom? (we still have most of them . . .), (3) funeral – how to do?

The friends were glad to talk about Timo, to talk about his character and what he liked and what his views were and what he meant to them – why they loved him. He was fun to be around, naturally very entertaining with a wicked sense of humour. A good flatmate, a good cook, easy-going, easy to talk to, open-minded, gentle, honest, objective, did not push his opinions. He linked diverse people, he was intelligent, he was always ready to help, he was a loyal friend. Skateboarding was very important to him on a social and personal level. It was a non-competitive activity, it was about communicating with others and competing only with oneself, not showing off, looking for self-fulfilment, responding to one's environment in an individual and thoughtful way. Once he had decided to do law his sense of well-being had definitely improved.

I was overwhelmed by their feelings and respect. I knew he was popular, I knew he was 'good with people', but it went much further than I had imagined. These points would be made over and over again by these and many other friends in letters to us, in the Commemoration Book, at the Memorial. We felt very proud when we prepared our statements, not just for the police, but for the press, and much later, for the Crown Prosecution Service when the tariffs for the juveniles were being decided by the Lord Chief Justice.

Some of the friends were very sure which of Timo's possessions they wanted. An old friend wanted the *poo-bum* photo that he used to have on his desk (this was a photo of Timo at the age of eight standing next to a sign for the village of Poo, in Asturias, holding a packet of crisps labelled Bum; he had written 'FAT TURKEY' on the bottom). A girlfriend wanted the window box that she had given him, one of his flatmates wanted his scruffy green and white stripe dressing gown (we never did recover that), I wondered if we should give his decks and records to Gabe. No-one wanted the car.

Everyone was quite clear that the funeral should be non-religious. We were thinking about Mortlake Cemetery. Sam and I had not worked out then that we wanted to bury him at home. We also wondered about doing a Memorial Ceremony, and I suggested the Barnes Community Association Hall in Kitson Road; but that was felt to be the wrong place – the connection with the Drama Group would be too hard to bear. We knew we would have to wait a while because of the post-mortem, so there was no rush to come to any definite conclusions. In the event, we had to wait nine weeks for Timo's body to be released. We did the Memorial in July.

*Monday 21 June 1999*

Sue Bishop picked us up at about 8am to take us to the morgue. She had managed to arrange for us to see Timo in his clothes. This visit was obviously not strictly by the book and we were made very aware that they were very busy today. He was wearing blue jeans (the baggy sort), a T-shirt (grey?) and a sweatshirt (blue I think). The shirts were up over his chest, showing some midriff. He only had one trainer on. He looked more Timo than on Saturday night, but still ghastly and dead. We cried and cried. I shook hands with the morgue man and said thank you. Sue said he would cover Timo with a plain white sheet when we went back later in the day.

She took us to Hungerford Bridge and showed us where it happened, found the marks left by the forensic people. It's a long way down. The river is murky.

We went to Bow Street Magistrates' Court. Sonni Reid (aged 19) and John Riches (aged 21) had been arrested on Friday 18 June, and Alan West (aged 16) had been arrested on Saturday 19 June. Sue ushered us into the courtroom where they would be appearing. We had to sit through something else first. We met Detective Sergeant Graham Williams and Mrs Simms, the CPS lawyer, who found us better seats (away from the family and friends of the accused). The three looked cocky and made obvious eye-contact with those behind us. They would not have known who we were. Reid waved at someone, West waved at his mother. Riches did not look glum at this stage.

It was all relatively brief. They were not given bail. Despite attempts by relatives of Reid to offer him accommodation (he had been sleeping rough), they were all three to be kept in custody.

Carlton's *London Today* programme reported the hearing and mentioned the forthcoming inquest. They showed pictures of Timo's body being recovered from the Thames.

In the afternoon Sue took us back to the morgue to see Timo after Dr Ian West's post-mortem. Fan came too. Timo was covered with a plain white sheet as we had asked, only his head was on display. He looked much the same as he did on the first two viewings. Ghastly and dead. We cried and cried.

The front page headline on the *Evening Standard*: 'Three accused of river murder. Horror of student's Thames death fall.'

*Tuesday 22 June 1999*

In the afternoon we went to see the friend in East Dulwich. He was very distressed at the death of a new friend with whom he was getting on so well. His room was not very big. It was full of musical items, tapes, CDs, a ghetto blaster, books. He had packed all Timo's stuff. I could not work out how the two of them had managed to sleep in this tiny cluttered space.

A751 HLM was parked up the road. I was feeling stupid for having forgotten to bring the spare key. Timo's key was of course with all his belongings with the police. So we could only peer in. Later we would send a key to one of the friends, who would collect the car, deliver the contents to Fan and Nigel, and park it in Barnes.

*Wednesday 23 June 1999*

Sue Bishop collected us and Fan at 8.45am and took us to the inquest at the Elephant and Castle. Although the post-mortem was done at Westminster, the inquest had to be in the place where the body was found, in Southwark. Dermot Keating and Graham Williams were already there. We were put in a 'private' room until it was our turn in the courtroom. We were told that the inquest would be adjourned, and were warned that Timo's body might not be released for up to two months, as each defendant had the right to have her/his own post-mortem. The Coroner was Selena Lynch. It was all very brief, she passed on her condolences. We left by the back door in case there were any journalists.

Sue came in for a cup of tea and explained the next events. She gave us a green folder prepared by the Home Office, *Information for Families of Homicide Victims*. Detective Chief Inspector David Shipperlee was the person at the top, overall in charge of three cases at the moment. It was expected that the next three arrests would be made soon. The committal to the Crown Court should take place within the next four to six weeks, and the trial would therefore be in October. (And indeed, the committal was first arranged for Monday 23 August 1999. However, it was postponed until 7-8 October; and so the trial could not take place before January 2000.) Sue would come and visit us in Wales, to take our statement. The Coroner's next hearing would be after the trial, or not at all.

We spoke to Gabe. He was not ready to see people yet. Seeing the police tired him out.

So we went home. We piled what we could of Timo's belongings from Fan and Nigel's coal hole (they called it Limbo) into the car. We left behind the computer and the items we thought would be passed on to friends. There was not room for it all anyway. In fact, in the end we took everything else (except the computer which failed to work) on our next trip. In the end we wanted his stuff with us in his room.

We collected the dogs from Castlepride. At home were the beginnings of massive post and several messages on the answerphone. We made a pact. Do everything together. Open the post together. Keep the phone on answer. Take the dogs out together.

Exactly four weeks from today we would hold our Memorial Ceremony.

# Waiting for the Trial

The other three were arrested and kept in custody:

*Wednesday 30 June 1999:* Cameron Cyrus (aged 18);
*Thursday 8 July 1999:* Shaun Copeland (aged 14);
*Friday 16 July 1999:* Toni Blankson (aged 16).


*Wednesday 21 July 1999: The Memorial Celebration*

I wrote my first Timo poem for the Memorial. The Celebration was held in a church hall in Barnes. It was organised by Timo's friends. The programme consisted of music by Ornette Coleman, Aceyalone and Blind Willie Johnson, and spoken tributes to Timo from family and friends. There were blue and orange flowers, photographs, a Commemoration Book, tea and sandwiches. There were so many people there that we could not speak to them all.


*Wednesday 4 August 1999: Visit from Sue Bishop*

Sue Bishop and a colleague drove down to take our statement. She told us that if there were any convictions we would be entitled to claim compensation.


*Saturday 21 August 1999: The Burial*

It was nine weeks before Timo's body was released. We found a funeral director who understood our wish for a humanist burial on our own land. He knew someone who would make a wicker coffin. Close family, my best friend from Germany, and Timo's main friends, more or less the same ones who were there on that first Sunday after his death, plus a few more, came to the Burial. People stayed overnight, in bed and breakfast accommodation, in our spare rooms, in sleeping bags on sofas or the floor, in tents on the garden field.

*Thursday 7 October 1999: Committal*

The six were committed to the Crown Court.

*Thursday 4 November 1999: Plea and Directions Hearing*

We went to Court 11 at the Old Bailey for the first hearing. Sue Bishop met us (and Fan) at St Paul's tube station, took us into the building and generally looked after us, as she would do every day of the trial. We were introduced to the Crown Prosecution Service barrister, Jonathan Laidlaw. He told us that the trial was likely to last six weeks. We had seats to one side of the courtroom, underneath the public gallery. There were Judge Ann Goddard, most of the defence counsel and solicitors, and all six defendants. They looked so young, so harmless. Each one stood up in the dock and said 'not guilty'. Judge Goddard fixed the date for the start of the trial as Monday, 31 January 2000.

*Saturday 4 December 1999: A751 HLM*

It was not worth trying to repair the Polo. A Barnes friend had arranged for the scrap merchants to collect it on Monday. We removed the last of Timo's belongings and took photographs.

*Friday 10 December 1999: Planting the Grove*

Suleyman Mowat from our local tree nursery planted over fifty trees around Timo's grave. The grove was funded by donations from family and friends. Other donations went towards a memorial bench in Barnes and SAMM (Support After Murder and Manslaughter).

# The Trial

*Monday 31 January 2000: to West Acton*

The trial was to start a day late. We had arranged to rent a flat in West Acton for six weeks. West Acton is on the Central Line which goes directly to St Paul's. Martin and Denise, and then Kathy, a neighbour, would look after the dogs. If the trial really did last for six weeks they would have to go to Castlepride after that. The trial actually lasted nearly eleven weeks. After week six we moved to a flat in Ealing (also on the Central Line). Some weekends we went home. Fan or Nigel would usually come to the trial with us. Martin came several times, and Denise. Friends came regularly to the public gallery.

On that Monday Sue Bishop gave us copies of Gabriel's interviews with the police and the post-mortem statement from Dr West. She took us to Ealing Police Station to show us the CCTV videos. Grainy, indistinct pictures of Timo's next-to-last moments.

*Tuesday 1 February 2000: the Trial Began*

The trial had a false start. Members of the jury felt intimidated by friends of the defendants as they left the Old Bailey on their first day. The trial restarted on Monday 7 February 2000 with a new panel of jurors. Anybody going into the public gallery from now on would have to show identification.

Although she was not on bail, as a juvenile Blankson was free to walk about the building. In due course, after his mother complained, Copeland was given this freedom too.

Special arrangements were made for them in the courtroom. They would sit with their barristers in the well of the court, though they would have to be in the dock at formal moments. The day was shortened. The trial would be characterised by delays: submissions, legal arguments, defendants arriving late, defendants being indisposed. We had seats to one side of the court, often close to defendants' relatives, but had to be sure to contain all reactions in order to retain this 'privilege'.

The prosecution case was that each defendant was guilty, as least as a secondary party, in a joint enterprise of murder and attempted murder. The details of events came mainly from Gabriel's evidence and CCTV film.

On Thursday 17 June 1999 Timo and Gabriel had a night out in the West End. Early on Friday morning they were walking and skateboarding their way to Gabriel's flat in the Oxo Tower on the South Bank. They were crossing the River Thames by Hungerford Bridge as it was the quickest route. Just before 4am, as they got to the centre of the bridge, they were confronted by three muggers. Alan West grabbed Timo by the throat, hit him and threw his glasses in the river. He threatened to throw Timo and Gabriel into the river if they did not hand over their money. John Riches went through Timo's pockets. Sonni Reid kept Gabriel at bay and pretended he had a knife. Gabriel kept telling them that they had no money. West went through Timo's rucksack. Cameron Cyrus, Shaun Copeland and Toni Blankson came onto the bridge from the Charing Cross end. Gabriel called out to them: 'We're being mugged, can you help us?' The two groups knew each other. Copeland aimed a punch at Timo and missed, but he punched Gabriel so hard that he fell to the ground. Immediately Gabriel was being kicked and stamped on from all sides, until he lost consciousness. They did the same to Timo. They then threw Gabriel and Timo into the river, forty feet below. Gabriel regained consciousness and was rescued. Timo drowned.

The CCTV pictures show the six covering their heads as they left the bridge together at the Waterloo end. The pictures also show that they swapped clothes. Cyrus, Copeland and Blankson were laughing as they walked through Waterloo Station, Copeland and Blankson hand in hand; Copeland and Blankson kissed. Reid, Riches and West crossed back over the bridge. Riches and West assaulted another man at Charing Cross.

Because of the CCTV videos none of the defendants could claim they were not there; but each one denied involvement and blamed some or all of the others: a 'cut-throat' defence.

*Reid* was standing there. He was too drunk to kick. Mr Cornish just disappeared like a dream. Obviously he saw him disappear but he didn't know how. He wasn't sure where Mr Baxter was. Mr Baxter was not there. He couldn't remember it. He wasn't saying he couldn't see it, but he couldn't remember it. He hadn't a clue why he swapped shirts with West. He just wanted to distance himself.

*Riches* said the other three came and it went hectic. He was standing there. They were doing what they were doing. He had never seen anything like that before. He didn't see West strike anyone with a skateboard. Someone said, let's chuck them over it'll be funny. He laughed, he thought it was a joke. When they chucked Mr Cornish and Mr Baxter over he thought maybe they'll do it to him. The girl threw the skateboard in. He was gobsmacked, being sick, in shock.

*West* thought they would give them a good kicking then walk away. Blankson was egging on and laughing. She said, let's chuck them over it will be funny. Cyrus and Reid put Mr Cornish on top of the rail and dropped him in. He heard the splash of someone going in the river. Cyrus and Copeland threw Mr Baxter in. Blankson threw the skateboard in. He thought it was sick. Reid sang 'Murder She Wrote' (a Ragga song about a girl called Maxie). He changed clothes with Reid to distance himself.

*Cyrus* was there to let the truth be heard. It was a mad situation. Copeland punched Mr Cornish in the face and he fell to the ground. Copeland, Reid and his two mates started to kick and stamp on him. He was not involved in that equation. He was trying to protect Blankson from this violence. Suddenly there was a splash and Mr Cornish was no longer on the bridge. He could not be 100% definite about who threw Mr Cornish in the river, as he did not actually see it taking place, but Reid and Copeland were by the railings. The next thing he knew they were attacking Mr Baxter, though he could not exactly say who did what as his view was blocked. He turned to comfort Blankson. Seconds later he saw Reid and Copeland release Mr Baxter into the water. He was shocked, numb.

*Copeland* went para. He hit the smaller one out of fear. It was just a punch, he didn't fall to the ground. Copeland wanted to hurry up and go where he was going. He saw Cyrus, Reid and the other two stamping on someone's ribs, Blankson was saying, yeah, do it, do it. He was trying to walk off the bridge. He heard a splash. He saw Riches and Cyrus pick someone up from the floor, put them on the railings and let them go into the water. Blankson threw the skateboard in. He was in shock, he didn't know what to do.

*Blankson* thought it was out of order. In her eyes there was no reason for it. They just done it. She had never seen anything like that before. She knew that the boys, they did like fighting and things, but she didn't think they'd go as far as murder, though. She was puzzled. She didn't think they could do something like that, especially in front of her. Copeland helped pick them up but didn't actually throw them in. West was a thrower. She thought it wasn't worth throwing the bodies over, bodies float. She didn't really think about what would happen to Mr Baxter and Mr Cornish. One did manage to survive. It was not true what others said about her egging them on. She was speechless, in shock, she was crying. Copeland put his arm round her.

She was asked to wear it and she done it. They were smiling at Waterloo because Cyrus was making jokes about vegetables. Personally she didn't even remember kissing Copeland at that time.

*Wednesday 12 April 2000: the Verdict*

The verdict was unanimous. The jury found all six guilty of the murder of Timo and the attempted murder of Gabriel.

Sam read out our prepared statement in front of the television cameras.

*Thursday 13 April 2000: Home*

We packed and drove to west Wales. We collected the dogs from Castlepride. They had been there far too long. It was a relief to be home.

*Friday 19 May 2000: the Sentence*

Judge Goddard said it was not possible to say who actually threw the two victims into the river. But she was satisfied that all of those convicted, apart from Blankson, kicked both victims, and that Blankson wilfully encouraged the attack; all six knowing there was a real possibility that the victims would be thrown into the darkness below. 'This was heartless, gratuitous violence for which you all bear a responsibility.' She described the indifference to the victims' fate as 'a dreadful feature of your conduct'.

She sentenced Reid and Cyrus to custody for life for the murder and 16 years' detention for the attempted murder; Riches to life imprisonment and 14 years' imprisonment; West to be detained during Her Majesty's Pleasure and 16 years' detention; Copeland and Blankson to be detained during Her Majesty's Pleasure and 12 years' detention.

# After the Trial

*Sunday 18 June 2000: First Anniversary of Timo's Death*

We took the gravestone down to the grave, a piece of rough slate engraved with *we love you,* prepared by Richard Boultbee of Llangolman. It is a replacement for the three small pieces of slate left on the grave by some of the friends at the burial. When Fan and I did our first plant, of thyme, oregano, cowslips, bulbs we lost all but one.

*Monday 24 July 2000: Juveniles Named*

Until this point publication of the names of the three defendants who were juveniles at the time of the murder (West, Copeland and Blankson) had been forbidden. After representations from the press, Judge Goddard lifted this restriction.

*Monday 22 January 2001: Claim for Compensation*

We sent our application for compensation to the Criminal Injuries Compensation Authority.

*Monday 14 – Wednesday 16 May 2001: Filming the Television Programme*

Sarah Macdonald and Kirsty Cunningham had been commissioned by the BBC for a series about youth crime. We agreed to take part in a documentary about Timo's murder. As a result we got to know Paula and Nate, who were also in the film. Paula was a relatively new friend of Timo's. She had known him for ten months and was devastated by his murder. She named Nate after Timo: Nathan Leonard Timo. (Timo was not the father.)

*Saturday 7 July 2001: Barnes Bench*

The memorial bench for Timo was installed in Barnes. It was organised by his friends, as their personal memento. The inscription reads: 'In loving memory, Timo, 1975-1999'.

*Monday 16 – Tuesday 17 July 2001: the Appeals*

The appeals were heard by three judges at the Royal Courts of Justice and were dismissed.

*Tuesday 31 July 2001: the Judgement*

The judgement at the Court of Appeal was handed down in a twenty-page document. Judge Goddard's 'exercise of discretion was unimpeachable', her sentencing was 'entirely appropriate'.

*Saturday 18 August 2001: Memorial Seat for the Grove*

We asked our talented local blacksmith, Eifion Thomas (who was born in the same year as Timo) to make a memorial seat. It is made of hardwood and galvanised steel. Eifion has fashioned a landscape and figures in an asymmetrical design, interpreted from our specifications. He delivered it in time for the second anniversary of the burial.

*Tuesday 8 – Friday 11 January 2002: Woodland Planted*

Woodland Management (Wales) planted 1,500 young trees, each about 50cm tall, in Timo's field; in time for his twenty-seventh birthday.

*Saturday 13 April 2002: the Tariffs for the Adults*

We were informed that the tariffs for Cameron Cyrus, Sonni Reid and John Riches had been set at fourteen years.

*Thursday 9 May 2002: 'Murder on Hungerford Bridge'*

The first documentary in the series 'Crime Kids' was shown on BBC2.

*Wednesday 18 September 2002: First Episode of 'Real Bad Girls'*

A six-part documentary series about Bullwood Hall Prison, made by September Films for ITV, was broadcast in September and October 2002. Toni Blankson appeared in three of the episodes.

*Thursday 15 May 2003: Death of Hermann*

The Beagle, Hermann, was found to have incurable bone cancer and was euthanized at the age of ten years.

*Thursday 19 June 2003: the Tariffs for the Juveniles*

We were informed that the Lord Chief Justice had set tariffs of ten years for Toni Blankson and Shaun Copeland, and fourteen years for Alan West.

# POEMS AND PROSE

## Die Them

Die them in the river
Die them
Die them in the river
Whoops over the rail.

Take off the glasses and
Chuck them
Chuck them in the river
Whoops over the rail.

Hold this can of beer won't
You don't
Spill it or you'll be chucked
Whoops over the rail.

Give us your skateboard you
Fucker
Fuck it to us or you're
Whoops over the rail.

Bash them punch them kick their
Heads in
Chuck them in the river
Whoops over the rail.

Die them in the river
Die them
Die them in the river
Whoops over the rail.

# Waiting For The Body

You identify your son's body. Timo's body. It is behind a glass screen. You may not touch. He is covered in a purple drape. Somehow that offends you – you thought you would see him in his clothes, as he was found. You have a caring Police Liaison Officer; she arranges it. You are numb. You think, when you get him home, you can dress him in clean jeans, T-shirt and sweatshirt, and two trainers. You shake hands with the morgue attendant, say thank you.

You understand about the post-mortem, you are all in favour. Three persons have been caught, justice must be done. You see Timo for a third time. His body is covered by a plain white sheet, as you had asked. He is still behind the glass screen. When you get him home, you will be able to look, touch, kiss him.

Three more persons have to be caught. This takes four weeks. You understand that the six defendants have the right to have their own separate post-mortems. You feel queasy about Timo's body being tampered with again. But justice must be done. Two further post-mortems are carried out.

You are still waiting for Timo's body, to have him home and bury him in the wicker basket at the end of the far field, near the cliff top. You have to wait nine weeks altogether. The funeral director tells you that you will not recognise him. He is skin-slipped, black. Sam goes to the funeral parlour, dares to look. He comes home, tells you Timo is a mummy.

You are cheated. You have Timo home, ready for the burial ceremony. He is in the wicker coffin, flowers all round it, in the quiet room with the curtains closed. The funeral director has put his clothes in the coffin as you requested; he gives you a small lock of hair. You cannot look, or touch, or kiss your son. You have to open the French windows.

## *Nine  = A Mummy*

Nine months of waiting for the labour ward:
induction drip and practise breathing, wet
the sheets and shiver, epidural, sweat
and pant, the forceps – have I got the hoard
of Babygros, the nappies in the cupboard
– lotion, talc to keep him smelling nice? Frets
with jaundice, colic; Mummy's weariness.
She wraps him in the pram; looking forward . . .

Nine weeks of waiting for the body so
we could lay you in the wicker coffin:
thawed, stinking mummy, skin-slipped, blackened. Though
you couldn't be dressed, we put in the ginkgo
sweatshirt and the spare glasses. The aspen
poplar quivering over you Timo

## *T... B .......*

Committed
to the
Criminal
Court,

due to a
very
serious
charge,

TB swans
around
the café.
I

am insulted.

## No Talking

Who not to talk to:
    any defendant;
    any defendant's wig;
    any defendant's social worker;
    any defendant's security officer.

If you talk, the wig will
    tell the clerk, who will
    tell the usher, who will
    m o u t h   i t   l o u d.

Remember:
    no talking.

## 4

On the footbridge that is 400 yards long they lifted us over the 4-foot high railings and threw us into the river 40 feet below.

At 4.09am Timo's alarm clock stopped.

## *Beginning with F*

I don't care if a young offenders'
institution beginning with F
is overcrowded,
has lavatories without doors,
is understaffed,
locks them in their cells
for most of the day,
has no training,
> work,
> education,
> or exercise,
and some of them commit suicide.

If you are in that institution –
> SR,
> JR,
> AW,
> or CC,
(SC is not old enough,
TB is female) –
if you are in that institution –

I don't care, I say
> F
to the lot of you,
> F-ing suffer,
F-ing suffer in F-ing Feltham.

## Specs

I bet you were an infant bully
with ideas about vulnerability –
skunks wearing glasses particularly.
Instead of ABC you learnt the tricksy
four-eyed optic fixation.

You grew into a pocket-picking
Vertical Volume Drinker (Male), jacking
punks at Waterloo, Embankment, Charing
Cross and Leicester Square, ABH mixing
it with tactic equation.

Mentally Styx one night, Mr Fix-it
Psycho plies his juvenile tricklet
with four machismos and a nixie chicklet.
The grievous, brainsick, Maxie sextuplets
earn a lifer conclusion.

## *You*

are not my aging stepfather
nor my Alzheimer-y mother
nor my three-quarters blind diabetic brother
nor my ninety-year-old stroke-bound aphasic aunt.

You
are my dead son.

*Timo aged 2.*

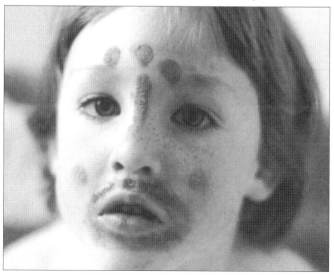

*Face paints from the Barnes Fair, July 1979.*

*Superman, Christmas 1979.*

*Brittany, August 1983.*

*Sam and Timo off for a 2-day trek in the Picos de Europa,
Spain, August 1987.*

*Aged 14.*

*Corin, an old shepherd, in Shakespeare's 'As You Like It', April 1990.*

*The last time he came on holiday with us, Brittany, July 1992.*

*With Hermann and me, Barnes 1995.*

*The last time we saw Timo alive.*
*At our home in west Wales, Easter 1999.*

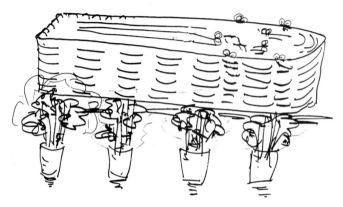

*Timo's wicker burial basket.*

*Timo's grave, summer 2000.*

*Timo's friends' memorial bench in Barnes, July 2001.*

*The memorial bench made by Eifion Thomas, in Timo's field near his grave, August 2001.*

*The woodland in Timo's field, 2002.*

*The woodland seen from the far end of Timo's field.*
*His grave is to the left.*

# First Anniversary

At four o'clock this morning we went down to Timo's field. It was just light, you could see the track well enough. Sam carried the bucket of white daisy chrysanthemums and I carried the gravestone. We had decided not to go to Hungerford Bridge for our vigil, not to throw our flowers into the Thames. Timo was after all not lost in the river; we had him with us, in the dell at the end of the far field, near the cliff top. The piece of slate fitted very well in the dip Sam had dug yesterday – just in front of the aspen poplar. We put the daisies next to it in a green pot.

I thought about how Timo had been dead for exactly a year, although we did not know at this time on Friday 18 June 1999. We did not know for certain until the Saturday. The anxiety began at around 2pm on the Friday when the policeman came to say that Timo was missing. When he still had not been found by the next morning he had to be dead. His body was recovered from Gabriel's Wharf that afternoon. That night we identified him at the morgue in Westminster. So the anniversary of our knowing does not really start until tomorrow.

I thought about the burial. I had stood at the foot end, where I made my speech, where I put my signed letter into the box which went on top of the basket, where I scattered orange and blue and white and yellow flowers into the grave, where the Ginkgo biloba was now growing. I had stood a few yards away at the head end, while Mr Jones and Mr Draper shovelled the soil back into the grave, while Mr Draper dug a hole for the aspen poplar, while people put the bouquets on top.

I walked among the fifty-two trees, and looked at the thriving new alpines that Fan and I had planted on the grave the other day.

The grass was wet. Lots of birds singing. The dogs were very good.

## No More

Eleven weeks in court. Defence is cut-
throat. Legal arguments. Forensics. Lies.
Closed-circuit tapes. 'OK, so I was there, but . . .'
Verdict: guilty. Willed joint enterprise.

I'll not forgive those six small bits of squeaking
arse-pit, devilfish that found it fun
to chuck two strangers in the river, wreaking
callous violence, murder on my son.

No more phone calls, no more visits back and
forth, goodbye the future altruistic
lawyer, grandchild holding granny's hand
so tight. In Timo's field I search for mystic

truth; plant thyme, aubrietia, snowdrops, tête-
à-têtes. *We love you* carved upon the slate.

## *Would've*

Amy didn't come today, my
daughter-in-law, the mother of my
grandchildren: who would've made houses
in the bracken in the fields, had
ponies, would've gone boating down at
Cwm-yr-Eglwys (god! and water-
skiing down at Aberfforest).

I would've taken them to Henllys,
the candle shop and the cyber
café, would've been forced to join the
Dinas Regatta Committee,
make cakes, do the barbecue, judge
sandcastles. Timo and Amy
would've been doing their sensuous thing

together. Doggies would've played hide-
and-seek in the orchard (Dizney
in charge) while I would've collected
the fish and chips.

## Plans

You were not two, or ten, or black.
You were not a little girl, or
a television presenter.
You were a twenty-four-year-old
skating philosopher,

                planning
to spend the night at Gabe's in the
Oxo Tower, then on Friday
visit the College of Law, and
on Monday drive down to west Wales
 to see your Mum and Dad.

You and Gabe had been socialising
with a couple of drinks at
One O One and Break for the Border.
At closing time you made your way
to Hungerford Bridge together.
Perhaps you talked about your joint
application for an Oxo flat.

At about 4.30 on that
Friday morning Gabe was rescued
from the River Thames near Millbank.

You made it to Gabriel's Wharf
on the Saturday.

## Timoträume (1)

Our old house. Edwardian.
Favoured residential road.
Detached. Corner position.
Walled gardens. Square bay windows.
Four bedrooms.

            *It's night. Timo*
*comes into our room. I watch*
*him walk over to the bay.*
*There are no curtains. Brown boards*
*seal each window. I see him*
*take a board and pull it down,*
*open the window and jump.*

*Or do I see him pass through*
*the boards, the windows, pass through?*
*I hear a thud – do I?*
*I go down the stairs, go outside.*

*No front garden. No garden wall.*
*No pavement. No road. There is*
*a dead body on the concrete.*

# Timoträume (2)

*A concert in a café*
– is it 'Break for the Border'?
*The programme: a small piece of*
*paper, handwritten. Or typed?*
*Six items? Mine is second.*
*Number two. For Linda.*

*Timo sings. Golden, lilting,*
*vibrant . . . Is that a lion*
*strumming the guitar? A wolf*
*rattling the tambourine?*
*And is that Francis jamming*
*on the tenor saxophone?*

Timo's voice. His melody.
We have no recording.

# Timoträume (3)

## 4am Dream

*He is sitting in a room.*
*A browny grey room.*

A scruffy, undistinguished, cheap-to-rent bedsitter.
There is no phone.

*He just sits there, still, silent.*
*His face does not move.*

A passive, listless, spiritless, lifeless, absent face.
A blank body.

*He is alone. On his own.*
*He has nothing to say.*

No Gabriel. No friendly phantom. Amnesia.
A damaged brain.

*I do not know where this room is. I have no address.*
*Unable to*

> *find him*
> *see him*
> *touch him*
> *talk to him*

I have to wait for him to contact me.

# *Vigil*

Standing sentinel
on Hungerford Bridge,

silently gazing
at the River Thames –

sombre, shadowy
reservoir of death.


Sensing figures in
the shroud of half-light,

silhouettes; seeing
a scenario

of mindless, vicious,
callous devilry.


Sitting on the rails.
Staring. Conscious. Drop

my glasses down – soft
focus. I let go.

Floundering. Dead wood.
Drowning. Dead skateboard.


Visualizing
what it was like.

# A Suitable Case for Dangling

We have attached six ropes to the railings of
Hungerford Bridge at 4am this morning.
The six perpetrators will be marched here hand-
cuffed and the ropes will be tied round their ankles.

And one by one they will be dangled head first
over the edge of the bridge to wait for the
tide to rise ever so slowly. We will watch
the six squirm in the murky mucky water,

spitting at flotsam and jetsam, trying to
climb up the rope. One will cry, 'At least they were
unconscious!' – so if they manage the forty
feet, we will simply kick and stamp their heads in,

chuck them back down. What fun! Hypothermia
will begin to take hold; no invisible
demons will make them float. Not *one* of the six
small pieces of squeaking arse-pit will survive.

We detach the ropes from the railings, drop them
into the Thames. We watch twelve ankles and six
ropes as they slowly disappear beneath the
surface of the river, sinking without trace.

## Inkling a Seat

Remembering

your first sentence
Spotter Puff
riding up and down
Ribena, Marmite toast
footie, Jabba the Hutt
stick insects, gerbils
Asterix, Brittany Ferries
butterflies, binoculars
Leg of Mutton reservoir
jam jars, herons, grebes,
boring old mallards;
the great roaring river that
tickled Jumping Mouse's heart.

Red flower on your T-shirt
Picos, sunshine
skating the South Bank
scratching the decks
a whirly rapper
not any old whippersnapper
hysterical improv
Corin the cool
houseboats, backpacks
Garstang, dry ski slope
culinary cultivating
Bachelor of Arts
Ginkgo, video
Burdett, Ratbone

lawyer intention
talk to you soon;
if you would like to leave a message
please speak after the l-o-n-g beep.

A jokey mug,
a T-shirt saying
Puffin     nuffin.
Shorty's snowboard;
the skateboard is lost
in the roaring river.
Foreshore, Southwark.
Bench the Polo.

Magic tree on my windscreen.
Built to grind watch on my wrist.
Your walnut starts to grow again.
Jumping Mouse leaves the sweet sage patch:
the Spots turn him into
a Soaring Eagle.

# Message Box

*for Fan*

Treasures found in Canolfan Carningli:
an earthenware crock for our wooden spoons,
a pine settle for the hall; and lately,
a cash box, just like Granny used to have,

for the safe keeping of her L.s.d.
Black metal, with a brass handle and lock,
compartments for shillings, florins, guineas,
crowns, threepenny bits; bank notes underneath.

Every year there was a charabanc
outing to Royal Ascot. Clara went
with Bill, her best hat trimmed with organza
lilies, taffeta orchids or a silk rose.

June. Before her nap she telephones
the bookmaker: 'Half a crown each way, please,
on Sweet William at two, on Love-in-
a-mist at three, and at four thirty on Love-lies-bleeding.'

We brasso our box till
it shines. Put our farewell letters in the
bottom, our poems where the coins would
have been. No key; we tie it with a blue velvet bow.

## Nathan Leonard Timo

Nate is coming:

> Stair guard
> Window locks
> Bucket and spade
>
> Huggies
> Baby wipes
> Full fat yoghurt
>
> High chair
> Weetabix
> Total sun block –

Nate is coming.

> Bed time stories:

I write,

> Books,
> For T.

# Estuary

Cross the iron bridge, refurbished, pristine,
white. Grey heron stalking round the pilgrim's
stepping stones. The egrets – have they gone? Green
fennel hides a murky pool, temptation
for the Springer. Mudbanks full of rumbling
herring gulls and piping oystercatchers.
Past the lime kiln, through the field of lethal
ragwort, thistle clocks. A canopy of
ash and sycamore, then gorse and bracken,
blushing hips, dark sloes. Reach out to taste the
salty blackberries; look over to the
other shore, remember picking samphire
on the longest day.

*Rosie's house.*

Drop down
to the beach. Now you can see the boat club,
Parrog, marram dunes, foam breaking on the
sands, Pen Dinas, luminous purple sky.

*L'Aber Vrac'h.*
*Buried under a blackthorn*
*thicket, a casket of troubles safely*
*stowed away.*

The Beagle barks at someone
in a scarlet parka. Dunlin fly up,
black-headed gulls yelp, curlews whistle.

*Message Box.*
*Buried under an aspen*
*poplar, with the wicker basket. Poems,*
*letters. Goodbye Sunshine memories.*

I don't enjoy this walk any more.

# *Wigwam Pagans*

This is the notification
of your final award for an
incident date on 18 June
1999 regarding
Timothy Raoul Baxter (deceased).

As proper funeral accounts
certified as paid are lacking
I have determined that you are
entitled to a sum of X
pounds for these sad circumstances.

The calculation is shown overleaf.

## For Our Spiritual Warrior

Good planting weather.
A field of twigs – wands –
each with a cane and opaque rabbit-guard –
dwarf evergreens and
mini Christmas trees,
heeled into the soil. It took four days.

Betula, Ulmus, Quercus, Populus
tremula, Sorbus, Pinus, Corylus,
llex, Malus, Fraxinus excelsior!

He has a holly spear, a poplar shield,
a rowan spray to ward off devilry;
ash for shelter from the gales. He can turn,
sculpt, build cradles and boats, smell the sweetest
pine, talk to the aspen, whisper to the
winds; glide through oak's threshold to the light.

*Be not afraid:*
*one and a half thousand rune-staffs*
*safeguard you on your way.*

## Primroses

It's Spring on your twenty-seventh birthday
and it's only the middle of January.
The bulbs are coming up – even the tulips –
though the rabbits? field mice? voles? have eaten
the crocus bulbs on your grave. Yellow and
blue flowers were about to emerge too. Oh well. *Tant pis.*

We'll go down there today, take doggies on
leads (because of the horses) and show them
the woodland – which is a week old – and say
'Digging here – no! Digging there – yes!' and hope
for the best. I will tidy up your grave
garden, put some compost on plus some of
those 'Get Off' crystals, and at the weekend
I'll plant some primroses where the crocuses should have been.

## *On Visiting St Davids Cathedral*

Purple House of God. The Shrine of Dewi
Sant. And in this tomb an unknown priest,
his likeness carved in stone.

His likeness carved in stone – the hands of countless
pilgrims rubbed it bare. Pulse of the spirit,
elemental edge.

Elemental edge of granite jutting
out into the sea and sky; an Angel's
lucid hidden valley.

Lucid hidden valley, clifftop field:
a bed of periwinkle, thyme and thrift.
The aspen poplar whispers.

The aspen poplar whispers photos at
the house; beneath this earth, a box of words, and
Timo's wicker basket,

Timo's wicker basket.

# All The Things I Did Wrong

Not loving you when you were born
Not wanting to give up my time to a squalling baby
Getting an au pair who did not talk to you
Not liking the gerbils
Not having another child
Paying too much attention to Grandma
Not consulting you over *Emil und die Detektive*
Not standing up for you when your bike was stolen
Disapproving of some of your friends
(who said and wrote such wonderful things about you
                                   at the Memorial)
Being rude about some of your friends
(who said and wrote such special things about you
                                   when you were dead)
Not visiting your flats in Manchester (God I was ill)
Moving your family home
Not hugging you when you failed the driving test for
                                   the second time
Not buying you a flat in London
Not painting your room white


I expect I've forgotten loads more

## *In Our Hearts*

In our hearts
in meinem Herzen

dans nos coeurs
in meinem Herzen

en nos corazones
in meinem Herzen

i våra hjärtan
in meinem Herzen

sydämissämme
in meinem Herzen

hamare dil me
in meinem Herzen

yn ein calonnau
in meinem Herzen

in our hearts
in meinem Herzen

in our hearts
aus meinem Leib

## Some of Timo's Sayings

Fat Turkey.

Does anyone want to Luba?

And also, Monkey.

Rule of the Toast.

What you doin'? Man, I'm just ridin' on these fools.

The Duck Rabbit.

Wake up Muttley, because you're dreaming again.

Come on let's get parking.

Rincez!

Creeping on you fools.

Let's get with the shilsnilshilsnobilsno.

Oh yes, when I wipe off my sweat.

Please mind your head.

Oh shit! Another gasface victim.

Stop flexing.

Just a smokey boy, from the land of the lost.

Don't overfertilize.

Dear Timo

I think it's about time I brought you up to date with what's happened since you've been gone.

One of the first things I did after we buried you was tidy up your room. It was such a mess. All your belongings that we had collected from Fan and Nigel's Limbo and the East Dulwich flat and A751 HLM were piled up in heaps. I sort of knew where everything was, but I thought perhaps I should organize it in case any friends wanted to take anything as a memento. Though they have been rather reticent about asking – presumably they don't want to upset us. Several of them have copies of the poo-bum photo, and the window box has gone back to Leeds. What *did* you do with the green and white dressing gown? We mended your watch and I wear it all the time. Your clothes are all hanging up neatly in the wardrobe (apart from the suit, which Fan has got), with your bedding and cooking gear and bathroom items. I've put your junior books in the cupboard by the window and the 'senior' ones are stacked on the window sills. Your philosophy notes and essays and general business stuff are in that chest by the bed. The records and tapes and skateboarding mags and videos are stacked in their original boxes next to the decks and the speakers. The phone is on the table. The snowboard leans against the wall – out of proportion really. Maybe I should lay it flat.

We had to get rid of the Polo. Not worth repairing. I've put the magic tree in the jeep. Oh, and your walnut! I'd practically given it up. This fern was growing in the pot instead. Do you know, the appeals were dismissed (I'm getting a bit forward now, sorry about that) just over a year ago – and the bloody walnut actually sprouted! It grew very well for ages. It's dormant at the moment.

About three months after we buried you we got this chap from the tree nursery down the road to come and plant fifty-odd trees all around you (to keep the aspen poplar company!). I won't bore you with a complete list (I can't remember what they're all called anyway without the plan), but we've put in several more aspens, some white poplars, some downy birch, laburnums, Austrian pines, four Raouli beech – couldn't resist those (that's one each for me, Dizney, Hermann and Schnuss) – and a Ginkgo biloba which we've put at your foot end. All paid for by donations! Actually, loads of people wanted to send donations. Some money went to this organisation called SAMM (NB double M) (= Support After Murder and Manslaughter). They've been good to us. The School Council at Shene sent £300, and Harry collected £400 at Manchester. Other people sent money for the friends' bench. That's up now. It says 'In loving memory, Timo, 1975-1999'. It's on the towpath just opposite the turning into Gerard.

Fan has helped me plant your grave. The first attempt was thyme, golden oregano, cowslips, crocosmia, snowdrops, crocuses, grape hyacinths, dwarf daffodils. We've added all sorts since – aubrietia, thrift, periwinkle, primroses . . . I do have to keep an eye on it, replant from time to time. Only the other day I had to turf out some decrepit thyme. I put in marguerites and a blue daisy called felicia. The grove needs attention too. We seem to have lost five trees. You are exposed to the elements down there. I'm thinking of replacing them with white poplar – that's the one that fares the best. It doesn't burn for one thing.

We had to wait ages for the trial – till February. It was very long – nearly eleven weeks, full of legal arguments and very difficult to sit through, listening to how they did it to you this way or that way or the other way over and over again. The only way I'd ever thought they could do this to you was because you wouldn't give them the skateboard. But it turned out that the skateboard was not an issue. They just threw it in the river too. So I'll never understand it. The main thing is that those six small pieces were found unanimously guilty and the ones called 'adult' were given Life, and the juveniles are being detained at Her Majesty's Pleasure. We had to wait ages for the appeals – well over a year – and were expecting them to be long-drawn-out too. Amazingly they were over within two days – dismissed. Satisfying isn't quite the right word or sentiment, but it will do for shorthand. We heard a few months ago that the 'adult' tariffs have been set at 14 years. The Lord Chief Justice is still opining over the juveniles. Basically you can rest peacefully in your basket for a suitable while.

This isn't quite the right word or sentiment either, but to shorthand 'celebrate' we asked the blacksmith round the corner to make a seat for the grove. Do you remember him? He's the same age as you, and pretty talented. We gave him some ideas about the things you were interested in and things we particularly liked and remembered and things we used to do together, and he came up with this unique interpretation. The bit you sit on and halfway up the back is hardwood, a sort of mahogany colour. The bits he has 'fashioned' are galvanised steel, a silver colour. Along the top of the back is a landscape – mountains, trees, river, clouds, sun – with a butterfly, a puffin, a soaring bird. On the left (if you're sitting on it) and down to the ground are hops, vines, olives, walnuts, mushrooms. Underneath a stick insect, a gerbil, a mouse. On the right a cityscape – a deck, a phone, a skateboard. In the middle of the sun is a copy of the red flower from that T-shirt of yours that I like so much, and around it is written 'Timo 17.1.75 – 18.6.99 Our Red Bus'. OK, corny. Can't help it.

Your field looks brilliant now. Back in January we got these chaps from a woodland management firm (one would have to be a Tim, wouldn't he?) to plant a woodland – 1,500 treelets, each approximately 50cm tall. Looked fairly silly, I can tell you. They were just twigs, held up with a cane and a rabbit guard, apart from the holly and the Scots pine, which had to take pot luck with the Rags, Tags and Bobtails. Had a few gales and had to go round straightening up a few canes. Then spring came and leaflets started to appear. And the grass started to grow. Which was a good scene as it offered protection from the wind. All you really see now is grass, but it's meadowy grass, and if you peer you can see the little trees.

The woodland wasn't there when we made the film. They showed it in May this year. *Murder on Hungerford Bridge.* We got to know Paula and Nate. They were in it too. You never told us about Paula. She told us that when she first met you she spent three hours buying a pair of trainers from you in Ratbones. She was a skater then. You called her Betty. She was devastated by what happened to you. Some time later she found herself unexpectedly pregnant. She decided to keep the child, in memory of you. He was due on 18 June 2000. She called him Nathan Leonard Timo. His father wasn't interested in him; Paula brings him up as a single mother. And brilliantly, if I may say so.

Anyway Timo, the point is we've got to know them really well and are very fond of them. I feel you should know this. Here we have, Sam and me, a kind of substitute for you. Here is the 'grandchild' I thought we would never have. Here is a pretend daughter I can talk to. They've been to stay a couple of times already. We take Nate down to Cwm-yr-Eglwys to muck about on the beach, we walk about the fields and visit you. Doggies are amazingly tolerant, in fact Schnuss is super-friendly. We generally have a nice time.

Though not such a nice time on Wednesday 19 June. We decided to visit the new Hungerford Bridge together. They've closed the old one. The new one is on the upstream side of the railway, looking out to Big Ben on one side and the London Eye on the other. It's like four times wider than the old one, it's well lit, it's got these tilted white masts. You could call it elegant. It's the complete opposite of that seedy snicket the six small pieces threw you off. Apparently they're going to build a downstream one too. All a bit late in the day for us. We were there at low tide. Gabriel's Wharf hasn't changed.

I hope you don't think I'm betraying you. I'm not betraying you. You'll always be the most important thing that ever happened to me. I see what we have as an extended family, that includes you. I haven't let you go. You're there all the time, in your grove and woodland, in your photos and belongings around the house. Your room is always ready. It's the same clean bed I made up for you for that Monday when you should have been coming but were being post-mortemed instead. I pick up the phone from time to time, wondering if you want to say something. You can talk to me any time, you know. I'm always here.

We'll be properly together one day. I'll be under my Raouli beech next to you under your aspen poplar. And Hermann and Schnuss and Dizney will be under their Raoulis too. And Paula and Nate will look after us.

Meanwhile, I'll keep in touch, will write again. Speak to you soon.

Lots of love for ever
Mum

+S +H +Ss

PS: That poem we read out when we buried you – 'Do not stand at my grave and weep' – I've translated it into German. A different take? See what you think:

> Bleib doch nicht bei meinem Grab und weine;
> Ich bin nicht hier. Ich schlafe nicht.
> Ich bin die tausend brausenden Winde.
> Ich bin der diamantene Schneekristall.

Ich bin das Sonnenlicht auf reifem Korn.
Ich bin der sanfte Oktoberregen.
Wenn Du in der Morgenstille wachst, da
Bin ich das rasche leise Rauschen der
In den Himmel aufkreisenden Vögel.
Ich bin die glänzenden Sterne der Nacht.
Bleib doch nicht mit Tränen in den Augen;
Da bin ich nicht. Gestorben bin ich nicht.

X M

# POSTSCRIPT

## Thursday, 15 May 2003
## Hermann's poem

Hermann liked it here.
Coming over from Hayscastle,
he'd sniff and dig the garden field
in Beagle contentment.
Was always happy to ride in the jeep,
despite the boredom when she
shopped in Safeway,
went to those funny site meetings,
disappeared in those kennels labelled *toiledau*.

We'd go to Newgale,
dance around with sociable mutts,
investigate nosy junky rocks,
upset tourist grannies during the season.
We'd go to Plumstone,
pretend the cows, the sheep, the goats,
the pony trekkers were not there.

Dog walkers said,
he's a mind of his own.
Did not come when called,
would just look at you, deaf
to the whistle routine;
chunks of cheese sometimes worked.
He soon understood
the Soar Hill topography,
wandering skilfully –
when you weren't looking –
a gap in the fence, a badger track.

Rooting about in
our neighbours' gardens.
Barking at unneutered
black males, the Dobermann,
protecting his sister.

Keen on picnics, Wonderloaf
meant for the birds, last night's
bonfire barbecue, old
crisp bags, sarnie wrappers,
black plastic, snotty tissues.
Cuddling under duvets,
elegant throws.

Senior. Ten years.
Tumour. Analgesics.
Nibbles a strip of thin ham,
a Frolic, a few grams
of puppy turkey.
Strenuous breathing.
Dying depression.

Steroids. Perk up:
hop-along down the garden field,
down to the uncut haylage bit
behind the birdsitting fence;
sniff and dig the mole hills –
any tasty young in here?

Timo's field.
A grave for Hermann Raimex Kindle.
We wrap you snug inside your fleece
in Timo's old blue duvet cover,
smother your cocoon with buttercup,
red clover, lady's smock and sorrel.
You sleep beneath Fan's strawberry tree,
facing Timo and the setting sun.

## *Viewing*

Willow between windows.
Dark brown wicker coffin.
White ribbons, white lilies
wake and weep.

Willow between windows.
Light brown wicker basket.
Wistful, dewless wide-eyes
watch and sleep.

Windows between windows.
Log on Outlook Express.
Maximize, double click
the icon.

Delete Timo.
Delete Hermann.

Shutting down.

# APPENDIX

# *Curriculum Vitae*

## TIMOTHY RAOUL BAXTER

*Address*: Burdett Road, London, E3.

DOB – 17/01/75.

EDUCATION HISTORY
*The University of Manchester*
  September 1994 – June 1997: BA (HONS) Philosophy, 2.1.
*Richmond Upon Thames Tertiary College*
  September 1991 – June 1993: 'A' Levels – English A,
  Philosophy A, French C.
*Shene Comprehensive, East Sheen, London*
  September 1986 – June 1991: 9 GCSEs – 8 A grades, 1 B grade.

EMPLOYMENT HISTORY

FEB 1998–PRESENT    *Ratbone Skates, Oxford Street – Sales Assistant*
                    Skateboard hardware and footwear retail.
                    Ordering stock, operating till and cashing up,
                    customer service.

JAN 1998            *Hays Montrose Building – Site Labouring*
                    Manual work, use of power tools, team
                    working.

JULY–DEC 1997       *Ginkgo Garden Centre – General Assistant*
                    Customer service, stock control procedures.

SUMMER 1995         *Daytime Child Minder*
                    Entertaining and caring for children aged 8,
                    10 and 12.

EASTER 1995         *Marco's Wines – Sales Assistant*
                    Customer service, operating till and cashing
                    up.

| JAN–APRIL 1994 | *Seeboard PLC – Sales Assistant* |
| | Electric Retail, customer service, setting up |
| | credit sales. |
| OCT–DEC 1993 | *Waitrose PLC – General Assistant* |
| | Packing and carrying out service, shelf |
| | filling. |

LANGUAGES:  Spoken and written French, basic German.

INTERESTS

*Travel* – I have travelled extensively in Western Europe (France, Spain, Belgium, Germany, Holland, Greece) and Eastern Europe (Russia and Czech Republic). I have also spent four months travelling around India.

*Sport* – Skateboarding, Football, Snowboarding.

*Current Affairs*

*Music* – Hip Hop, Reggae, Soul, Blues, Jazz.

Member of amateur dramatic group The Barnes Theatre Company, 1988-1991.

# Acknowledgements

*Losing Timo* was originally my dissertation for an M.A. in Creative Writing at Trinity College, Carmarthen. I would like to thank my tutor, Menna Elfyn, for her help and guidance.

I would also like to thank my husband, Sam Baxter, and my sister, Sue Bates (Fan), for their support and encouragement, and my editor, Elin ap Hywel, for her care and sensitivity.

'That Red Bus Has Stopped', an extract from 'No More' and 'Primroses' have appeared in newsletters of SAMM (Support After Murder and Manslaughter).

'Waiting For The Body', 'Nine = A Mummy' and 'For Our Spiritual Warrior' have appeared in newsletters of The Compassionate Friends.

I read extracts from 'Die Them', '4', 'Waiting For The Body' and 'No More' in the BBC2 television documentary 'Murder on Hungerford Bridge'.

'Hermann's poem' has appeared in the Beagle Association Annual 2004.

All cover photographs, and all other photographs in the book, were taken by Sam Baxter with the exception of the following – photograph 3: by Nigel Rees; photograph 5: by Martin/Denise Baxter; photograph 7: by a member of the Barnes Theatre Company; photograph 9: by Sergio Sandes de Sá. Drawing 11: by Nigel Rees.

# Reference

The Judgement of Lord Justice Rose, Mr Justice Bell and Mr Justice Stanley Burton handed down in the Supreme Court of Judicature, Court of Appeal (Criminal Division) on 31 July 2001. This document includes a precis of the proceedings at the trial and details of the sentencing.

# Notes

1. The Poems and Prose section more or less follows the sequence of events.

2. 'Inkling a Seat': Jumping Mouse refers to the story *Jumping Mouse*, retold by Brian Patten, Puffin Books 1977, first published by Allen & Unwin 1972.

3. 'In Our Hearts': the languages are German (in each stanza), and stanza 2 – French, 3 – Spanish, 4 – Swedish, 5 – Finnish, 6 – Hindi, 7 – Welsh. The first eight stanzas say 'in our hearts/ in my heart'. The last stanza says 'in our hearts/from my body (womb)'. Thanks to Tarja Roffe for the Swedish, Finnish and Hindi, and to Menna Elfyn for the Welsh.

4. Thanks to Jutta Busch-Link and Robert Link for checking my German translation of the poem at the end of the last letter. This is the original English:

> Do not stand at my grave and weep;
> I am not there. I do not sleep.
> I am a thousand winds that blow.
> I am the diamond glints on snow.
> I am the sunlight on ripened grain.
> I am the gentle autumn rain.
> When you awaken in the morning's hush
> I am the swift uplifting rush
> Of quiet birds in circled flight.
> I am the soft stars that shine at night.
> Do not stand at my grave and cry;
> I am not there. I did not die.
>
> *Anonymous*